Where Does It Go?

LIGHTNING, SOLAR, AND OTHER ENERGIES

Written by Helen Greathead

Illustrated by Kyle Beckett

Gareth Stevens PUBLISHING

Every effort has been made by the Publishers to ensure that the websites in this book are suitable for children, that they are of the highest educational value, and that they contain no inappropriate or offensive material. However, because of the nature of the Internet, it is impossible to guarantee that the contents of these sites will not be altered. We strongly advise that internet access is supervised by a responsible adult.

Please visit our website, www.garethstevens.com. For a free color catalog of all our high-quality books, call toll free 1-800-542-2595 or fax 1-877-542-2596.

Cataloging-in-Publication Data

Names: Greathead, Helen, author. | Beckett, Kyle, illustrator.
Title: Lightning, solar, and other energies / Helen Greathead, illustrated by Kyle Beckett.
Description: Buffalo, NY : Gareth Stevens Publishing, 2026. | Series: Where does it go? | Includes glossary and index.
Identifiers: ISBN 9781482475814 (pbk.) | ISBN 9781482475821 (library bound) | ISBN 9781482475838 (ebook)
Subjects: LCSH: Force and energy--Juvenile literature. | Energy--Juvenile literature.
Classification: LCC QC73.G724 2026 | DDC 531.113--dc23

Published in 2026 by
Gareth Stevens Publishing
2544 Clinton St.
Buffalo, NY 14224

First published in Great Britain in 2023 by Wayland

Commissioning Editor: Elise Short
Editor: Nicola Edwards
Designers: Anthony Hannant and Gemma Steward

Printed in China
CPSIA compliance information: Batch #QW26GS: For further information contact Gareth Stevens at 1-800-542-2595.
Find us on

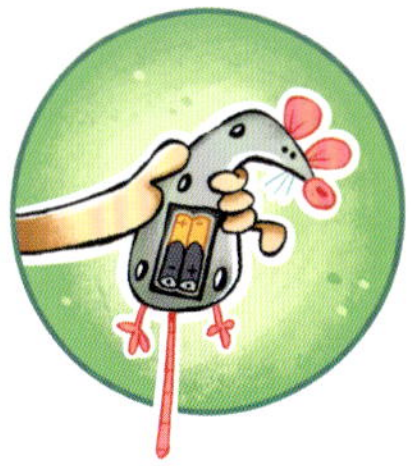

CONTENTS

What on Earth is energy? 4
Get moving 6
You've got the power 8
sunsational 10
Strike a light 12
Sky power 14
Prehistoric power 16
Gadgets galore 18
Going nuclear 20
All-day energy 22
Chasing the breeze 24
Water works 26
Farewell, fossil fuels 28
Glossary 30
Further information 31
Index 32

WHAT ON EARTH IS ENERGY?

We can't usually see it, but we need it for just about everything we do! Energy comes in lots of different forms. In this book we'll find out how these different types of energy provide the power to let things move, work, and grow. And we'll find out where that energy goes once we've used it.

These are just a few forms of energy and some of the things they can do:

Energy doesn't always stay the same. It can change from one type to another.

As the hot dog falls from the bun, it uses **kinetic** energy.

Kinetic energy turns to **heat** energy when it hits the ground.

Electrical energy comes from a power station.

1. **Heat** energy, for example from coal, boils water to produce steam.

2. The steam turns a turbine, which powers a generator that is made up of magnets and wires.

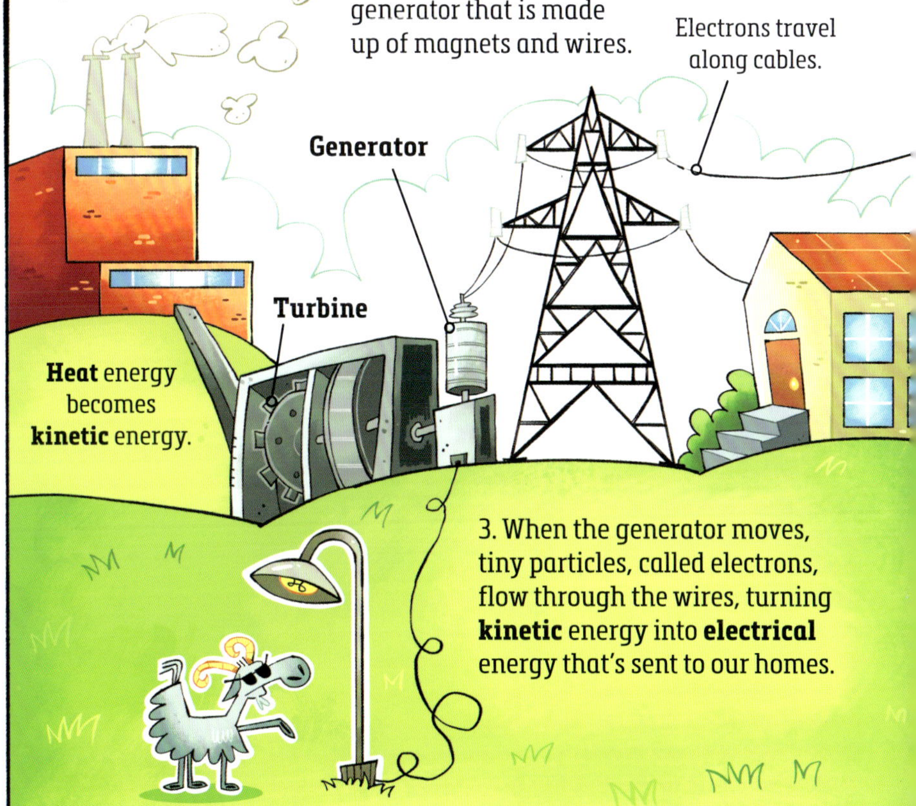

3. When the generator moves, tiny particles, called electrons, flow through the wires, turning **kinetic** energy into **electrical** energy that's sent to our homes.

The fuel that supplied the power station was an energy store. We can also say it's "**potential** energy," because we know it could provide energy even though it isn't at the moment.

So how is energy stored? And what is **potential** energy?

GET MOVING

Can you guess what this battery and this log have in common?

Believe it or not, they're both storing energy!

The battery stores chemical energy. That chemical energy can convert into kinetic energy, then electrical energy.

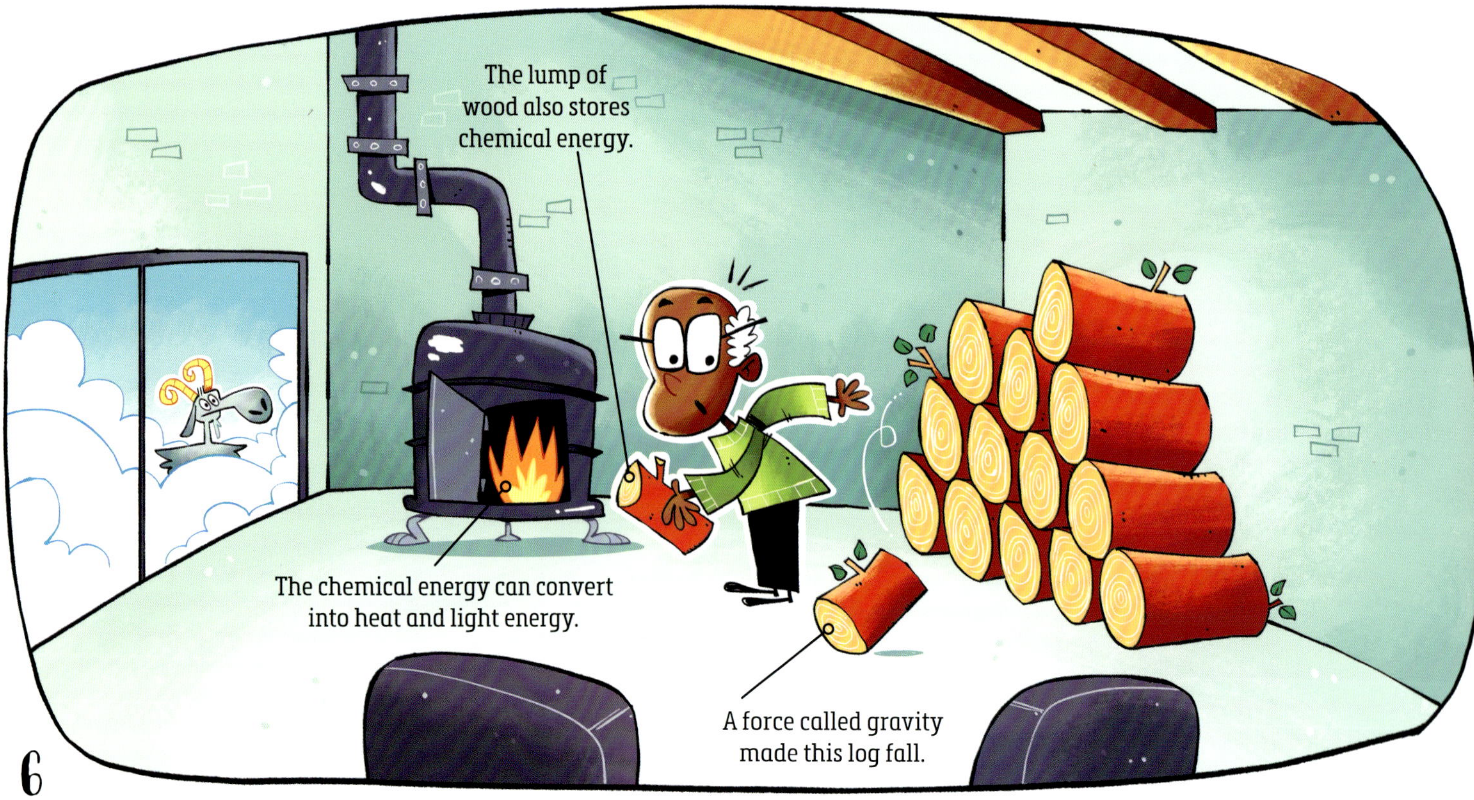

Gravity is a force that pulls objects towards the center of Earth.

Before the log fell to the ground, it was storing what's called "gravitational potential energy." Gravitational potential energy just means that because the log was quite high off the ground, there was a possibility that it could move with the help of gravity.

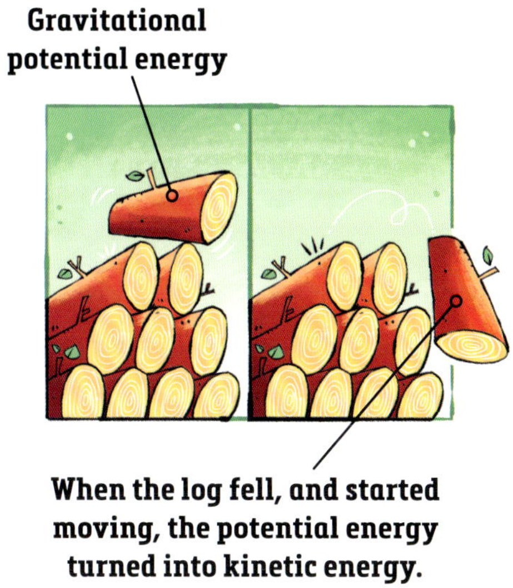

Here's another example of gravitational potential energy turning into kinetic energy. Check out these skateboarders jumping off a half-pipe:

All humans need energy in order to move, warm up, and even to sleep. So where does your energy come from?

YOU'VE GOT THE POWER

You and all humans get energy from food.

Yes, the food and water we put in our bodies contain the energy that makes our bodies work. From breathing to running marathons, everything we do needs energy.

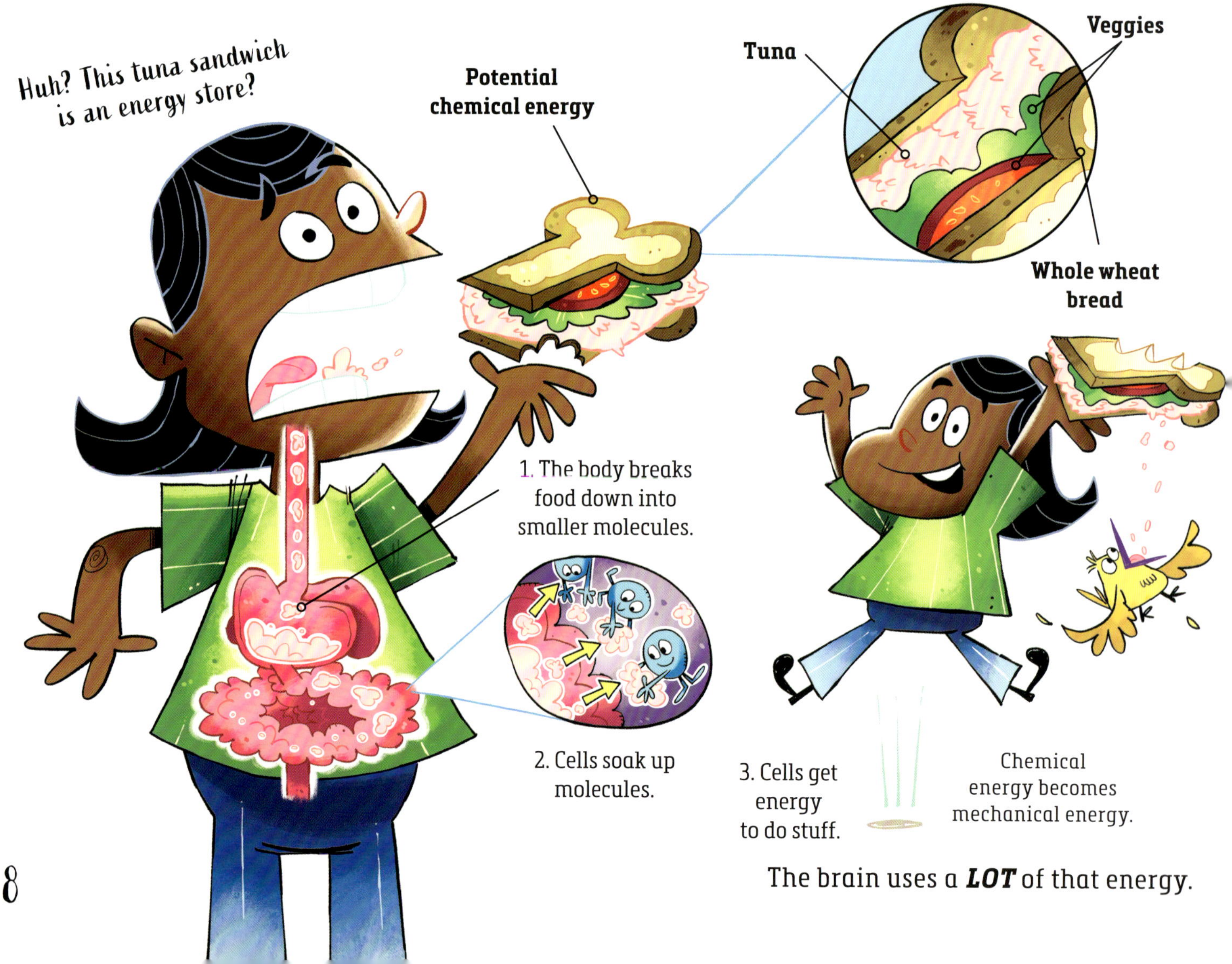

The brain uses a ***LOT*** of that energy.

A network of neurons

There are ***around 86 billion*** cells – called neurons – in your brain, which is where your body's decisions are made. Chemical energy converts to electrical energy to send signals pinging from one neuron to the next and instructions along nerves in the body.

Did you know ...
There's enough electrical energy in a human brain to power a light bulb.

Brain signals travel at speeds up to **320 kph**.

From sun to sandwich

So where did the energy in your sandwich come from? Animals (including us humans) get their energy from eating plants and other animals. Plants get their energy from the sun.

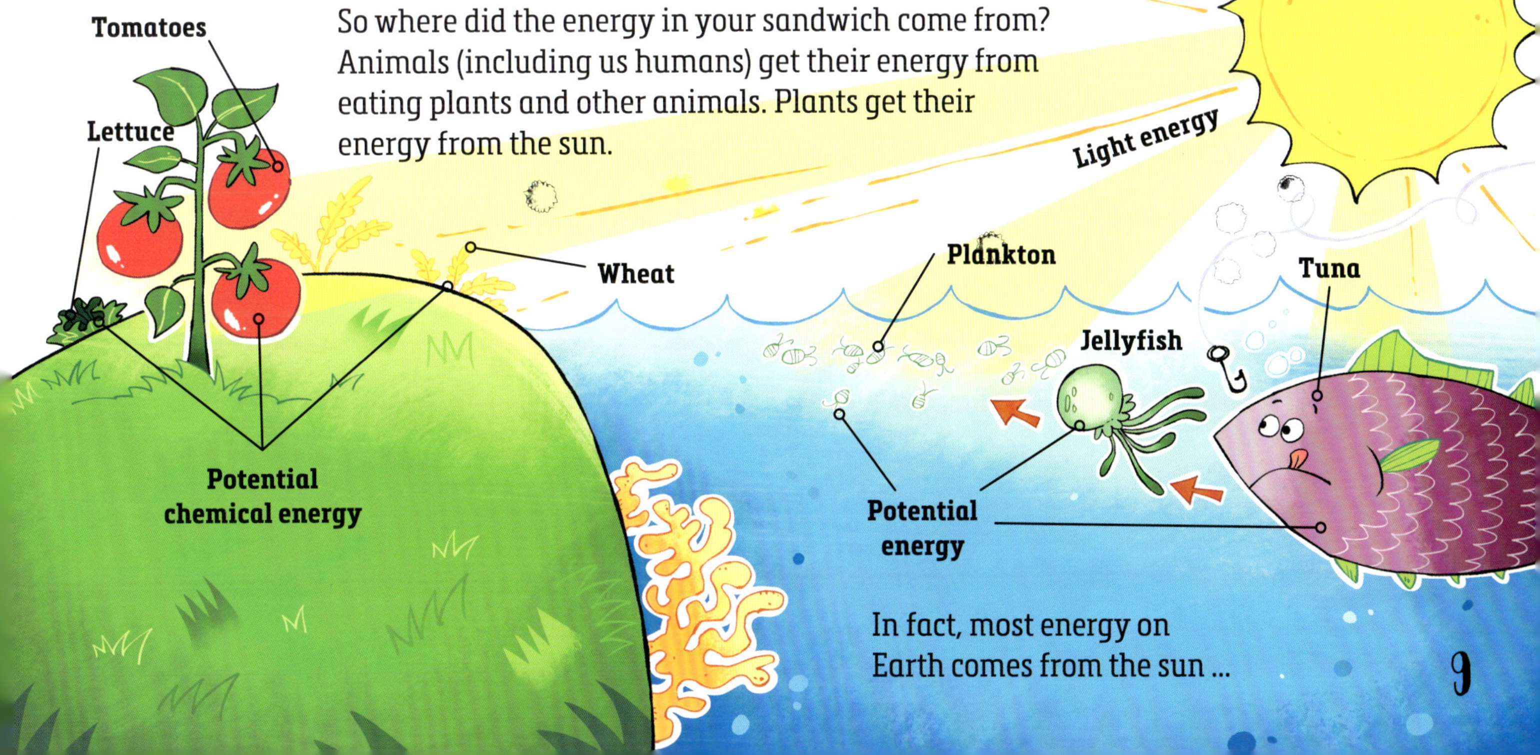

In fact, most energy on Earth comes from the sun ...

SUNSATIONAL

The sun, our nearest star, is actually **93 million miles (150 million km)** away! It's made up of hydrogen and helium. There would be no life on Earth without it. Our planet is in the right position to make use of the sun's heat and light energy.

It takes ***8 minutes and 20 seconds*** for the sun's rays to reach Earth.

The sun releases ***4.6 million tons (4.26 million mt)*** of energy per second!

Extracting energy

All plants, including plant plankton in the sea, use sunlight to create energy that they store as sugar. They do this through a process called photosynthesis.

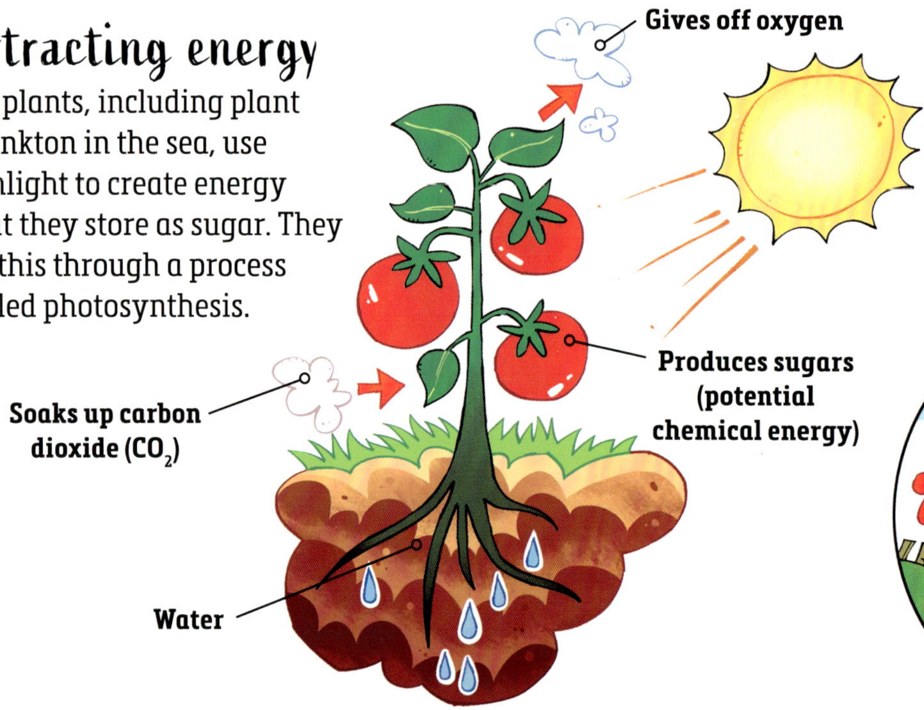

Animals that eat plants get energy from the sugars too. Animals that eat plant-eating animals also get energy from those sugars.

People were using the sun's energy for warmth and light long before there was an electricity supply.

- They got up at sunrise and went to bed at sunset.
- They dried food in the sun to make it last longer.
- They evaporated seawater to produce salt.

Six thousand years ago, some Chinese communities designed houses that used the sun's heat and light energy. Architects today use some of the same ideas to design houses that stay cool in summer and warm in winter.

But what did people do when the sun went down?

Humans have probably been warming themselves around fires for probably **over 700,000 years** – ever since they realized that they could extract the heat and light energy stored in wood, straw, seaweed, and animal poop.

How did people know about fires? Maybe lightning showed them what it could do ...

STRIKE A LIGHT

Imagine seeing lightning for the first time and not knowing what it was.

Lightning causes wildfires that destroy forests and wildlife. But it also creates heat and clears land. This made hunting and foraging for food easier for humans thousands of years ago. Some experts believe it taught people that cooked food tasted good.

As the planet gets hotter (see page 17), warmer air is causing more thunderstorms. When lightning strikes a tree, it can burn easily. Other trees quickly catch fire until a whole forest can be ablaze. These wildfires are hard to control.

But where does lightning come from?

It begins in a thundercloud.

Thundercloud

Ice crystal

Moisture molecule

Positive charge

Negative charge

1. Billions of cold ice crystals and warm moisture molecules rub together in the cloud.

2. They create static electricity (the stuff that makes your hair stand on end when you take off a sweater).

3. Just like a battery, the electricity has positive and negative charges.

- +

4. Increasing negative charges send an electric current racing towards the ground.

5. Positive charges from tall objects or the ground rise up to meet the current.

6. Lightning flashes until the negative charges are used up.

Did you know ...
There are ***50-100*** lightning strikes per second around the world today.

Did you know ...
The temperature around a lightning flash can be ***five times*** as hot as the sun's surface.

Could we catch the electricity from a lightning bolt?

SKY POWER

One bolt of lightning holds enough energy to toast **100,000** slices of bread!

In 2013, researchers at Southampton University, UK, created a fake lightning bolt. They used it to charge a mobile phone battery.

Could we power our homes with energy from lightning? Well, one company tried to make it happen in 2007. They soon gave up.

The trouble is, lightning ...

... happens too fast

... is too random – we never know where it will strike next!

Electrical potential energy from a storm cloud changes into light energy (the flash you see in the sky) and sound energy (the thunderclap you hear), but most of it becomes heat energy. A lightning flash can heat the air surrounding it to ***70,232°F (39,000°C)*** in a fraction of a second, but that heat is absorbed quickly into the atmosphere.

Did you know ...
Ball lightning is, well, ball-shaped. It might be as small as a pea, or big as a car. It lasts up to 20 seconds and can hover in the air, roll along the ground, or crash into people's homes!

... doesn't always hit the ground

... loses more energy as it gets closer to Earth.

Lightning's energy is practically impossible to capture, but there are easier ways to get power ...

PREHISTORIC POWER

Today, over 60 percent of the energy we use for heating, lighting, and to power machines comes from coal, oil, and natural gas. We call these fossil fuels because they're the remains of animals and plants that died millions of years ago. Earth looked very different then.

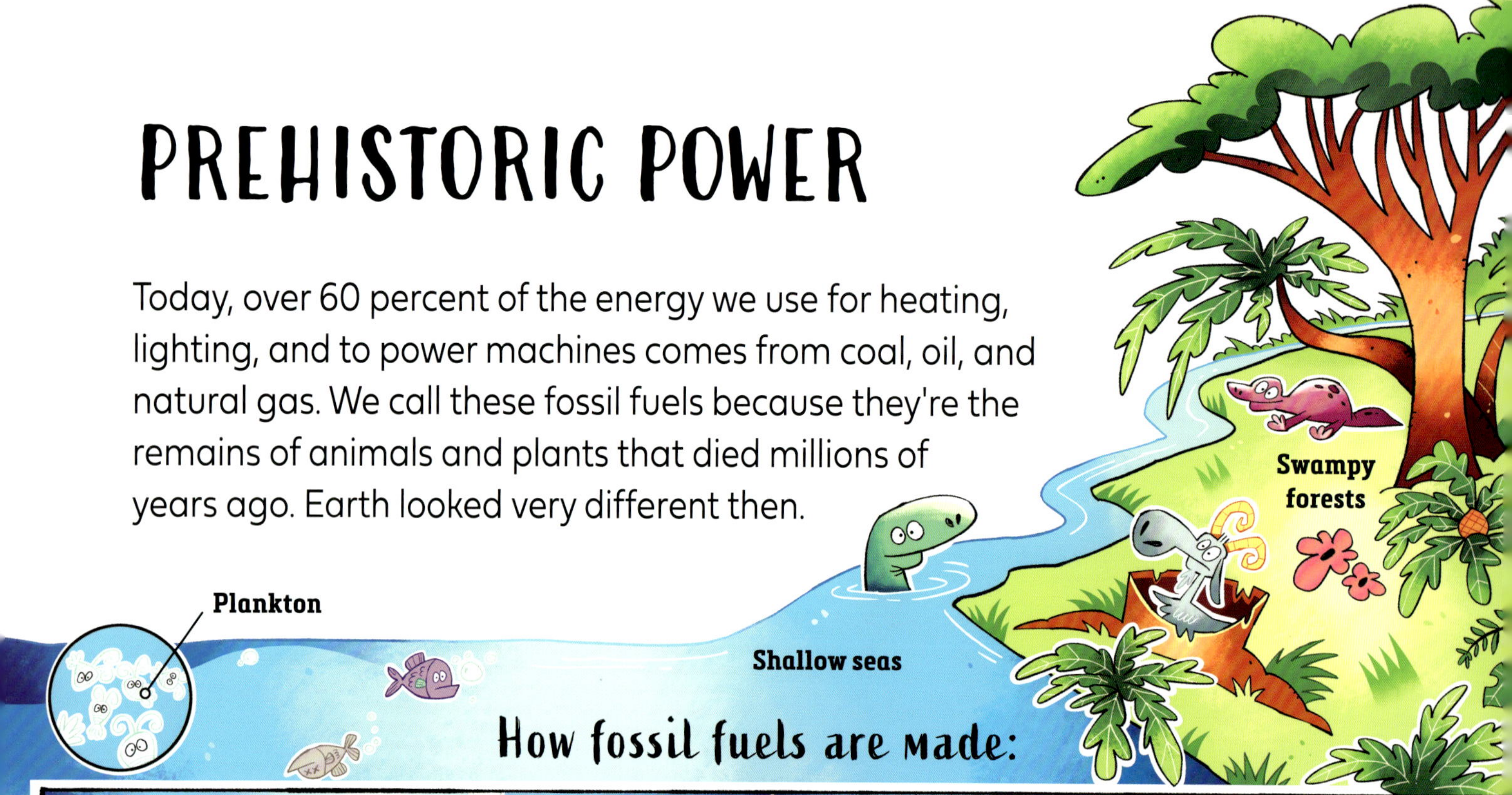

How fossil fuels are made:

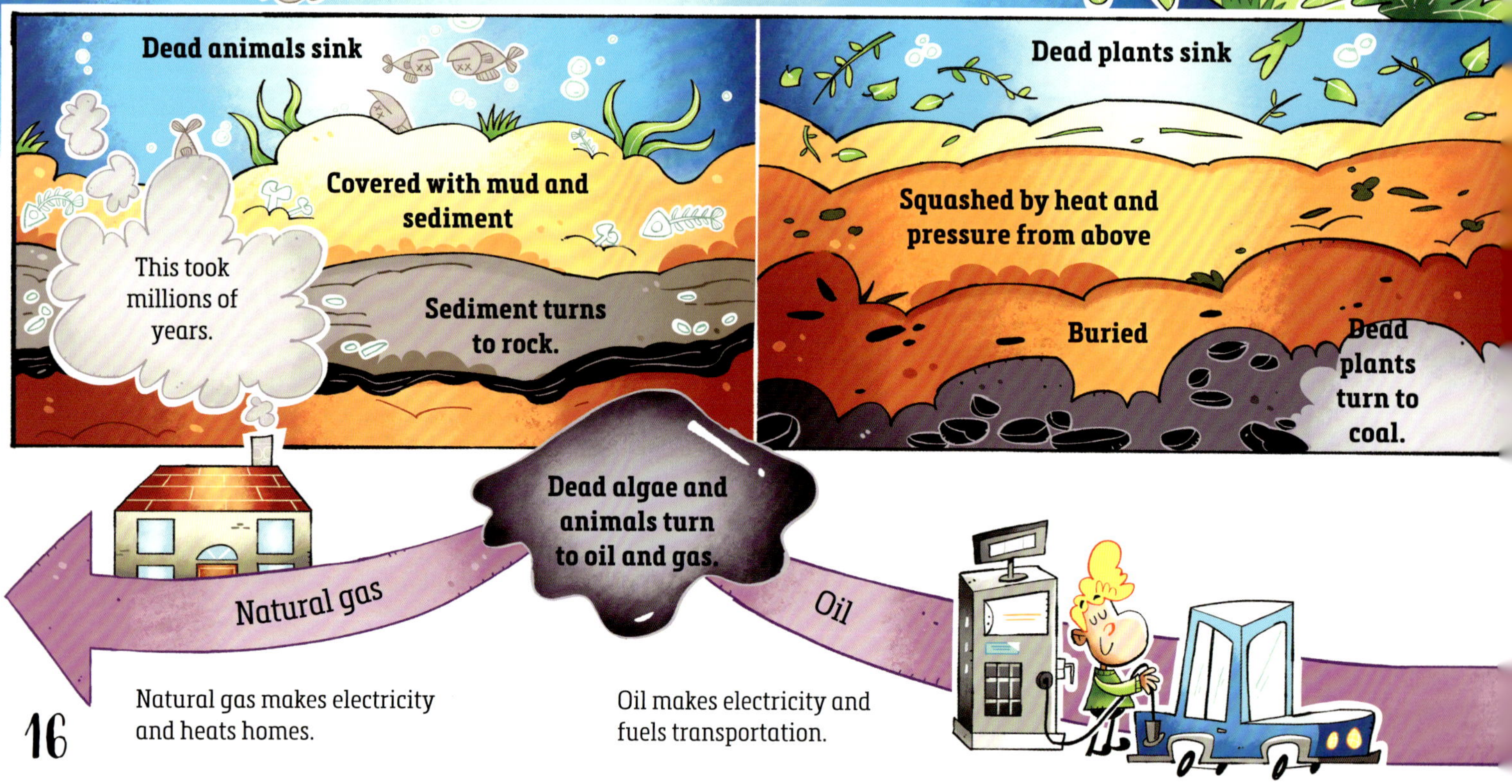

Natural gas makes electricity and heats homes.

Oil makes electricity and fuels transportation.

The problem with fossil fuels

When prehistoric plants and animals died, the CO_2 inside them was buried in the ground. Burning fossil fuels releases this ancient CO_2 into the atmosphere again – which is bad news for the planet!

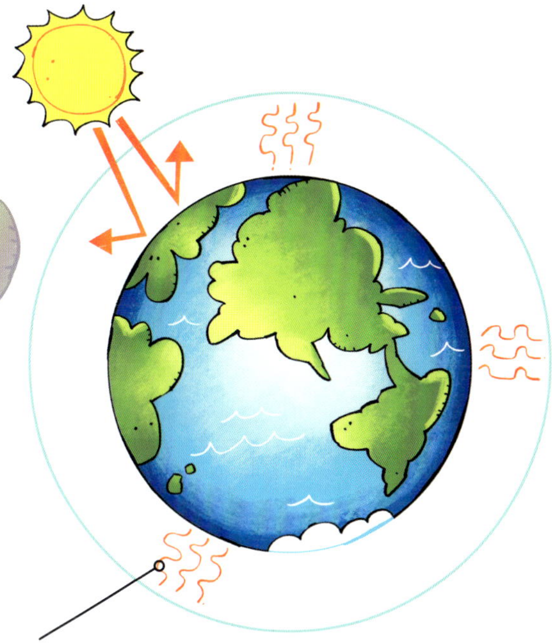

CO_2 is a greenhouse gas that traps the sun's heat to keep Earth warm. The extra CO_2 from burning fossil fuels is making Earth warm up too much.

Coal

Coal makes electricity.

Fossil fuels take **350 million** years to form.

We have been using them for **300 years**.

If we keep using fossil fuels, they will last another **30–70 years**.

We won't be able to make new fossil fuels fast enough if we do use up all our supplies. That's why we call fossil fuels "non-renewable" energy sources.

So how are we using all that energy?

GADGETS GALORE

Electrical energy travels along a network of cables to our homes, and it's amazing! Plug in a gadget or flip a switch and electrical potential energy will quickly transform into lots of other useful types of energy.

Satellite
Stored **chemical energy** becomes **mechanical energy** when this electric car drives away.
Battery
Cold water flows over a metal element to be warmed by **heat energy**.
Light, heat, and sound energy
Some TV shows are transmitted through a signal carried by a cable, satellite, or aerial.
Did you know ...
Most gadgets don't use all the energy they suck up. Sometimes they lose heat to the area that surrounds them. Gadgets suck up energy even when you're not using them.
One percent of world CO_2 emissions come from vampire energy.
You're wasting "vampire" energy if your unused gadget:
• has a light on
• feels warm
• is plugged in.
If our electricity comes from fossil fuels, then using gadgets is adding CO_2 to the atmosphere. Can electricity be cleaner?

GOING NUCLEAR

Nuclear power produces masses of electricity and **doesn't** release CO_2.

So how does it work?

Everything on Earth is made up of all sorts of different types of atom, which are held together with energy. The center, or nucleus, of an atom holds a huge amount of energy.

Because uranium atoms are easy to split apart, uranium is used as fuel. Splitting uranium atoms releases tiny particles that start a chain reaction creating nuclear energy.

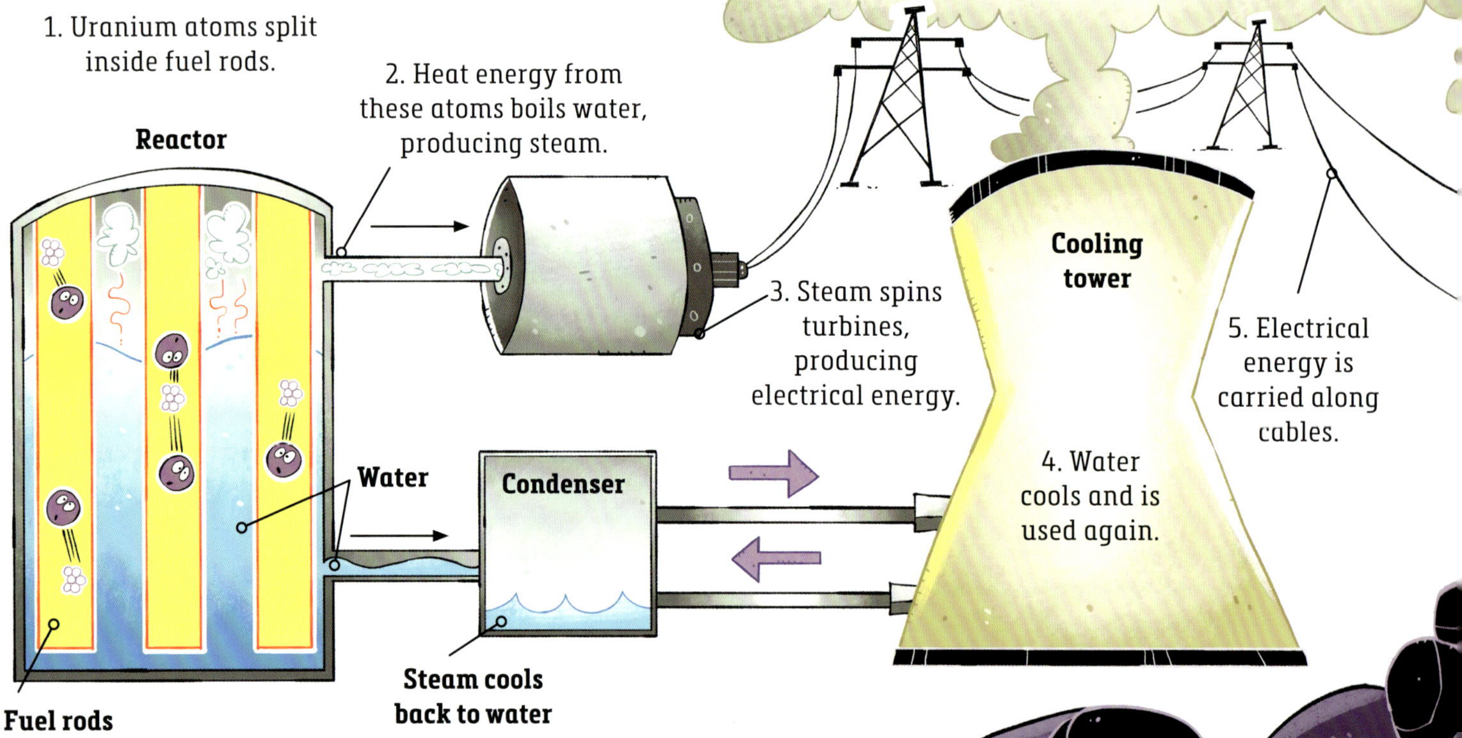

One uranium pellet produces as much energy as ***1.1 ton (1 mt)*** of coal.

Some people are really hot and bothered about nuclear energy...

Other people argue that...

Did you know ...

In 2011, an earthquake caused a giant wave to hit Japan's Fukushima Daiichi Nuclear Power Plant. The plant overheated, radiation leaked out and 47,000 people had to leave their homes.

Nuclear technology is improving and accidents are rare. It already provides 10 percent of the world's energy. But are renewable energies a better option?

ALL-DAY ENERGY

The sun beams down 5,000 times as much energy as we use on Earth each year. Because it shines every day, this "solar" energy won't run out: it's renewable. And it's clean, because it doesn't put out CO_2.

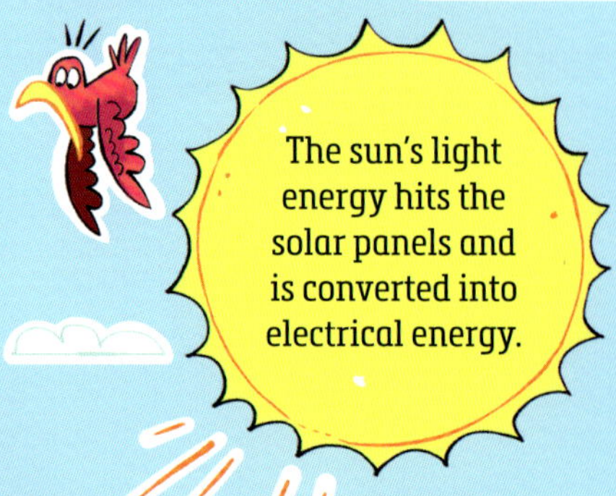

How sunlight becomes energy we can use:

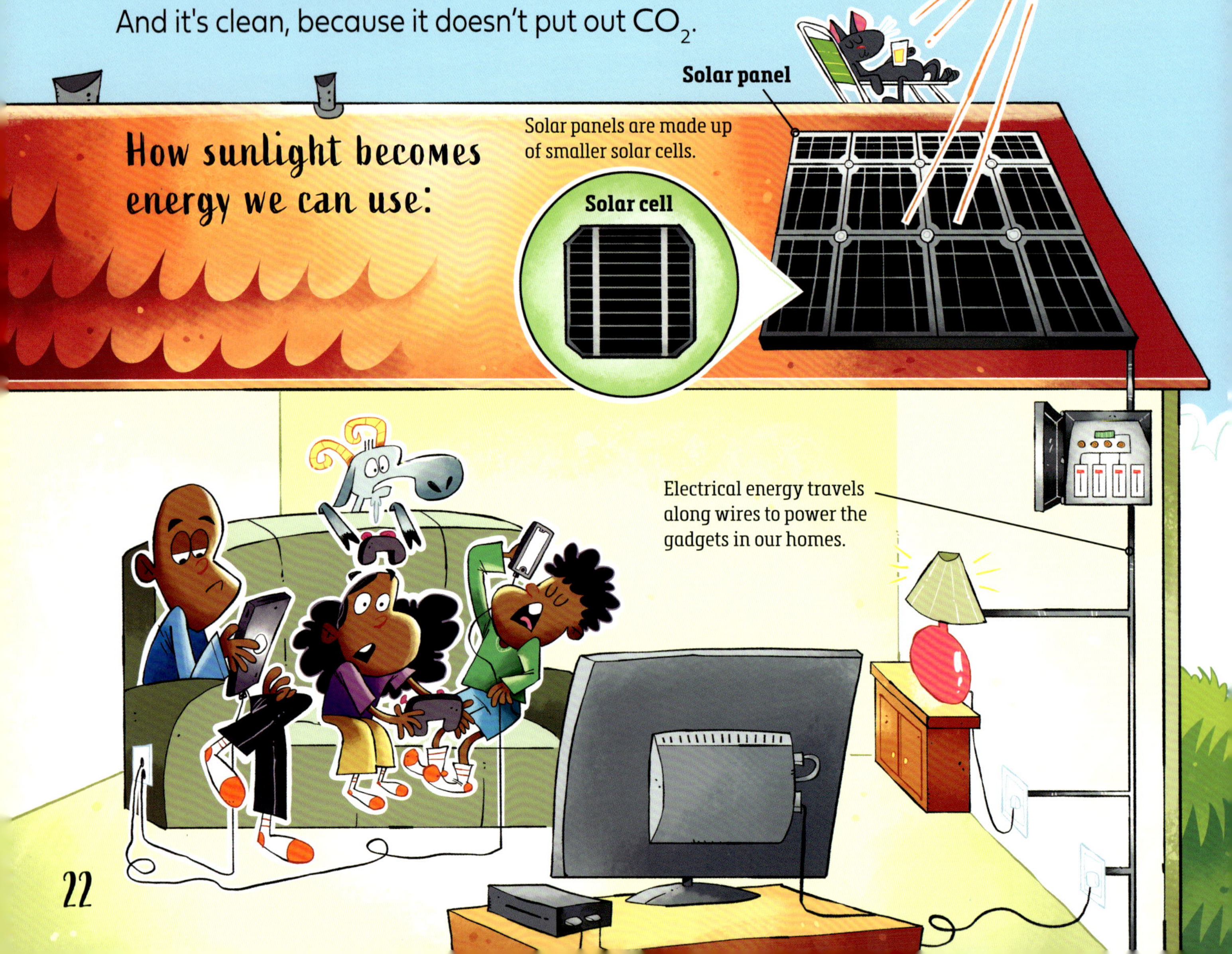

Sunshine farms

Lots of panels together make a solar farm. Bhadla Solar Park is an enormous solar farm in the scorching desert of Rajasthan, India. Rain hardly ever falls here.

There are over ***10 million*** solar panels at the park.

They feed energy to ***1.3* million** homes.

Solar panels aren't perfect:

- They can take up lots of space.
- They only work when the sun shines and storing the energy they produce can be difficult.
- Making them is expensive and uses lots of energy.

Some scientific solutions include:

1. Panels on stilts let farmers plant crops beneath them. The solar panels shelter the plants from heavy rain.

2. Short-term batteries, like the ones in a mobile phone, can store solar energy for a few hours, so that daytime sunshine can power nighttime activities.

3. A paste made from special proteins can be used to capture the sun's energy (see page 10) when it is spread on to simple solar cells. These cells would be cheaper and easier to make and could be used **anywhere** in the world.

Plant-paste panels aren't ready to use yet, so is there an answer in the wind?

CHASING THE BREEZE

Wind is air that's on the move. It's another source of energy that starts with the sun.

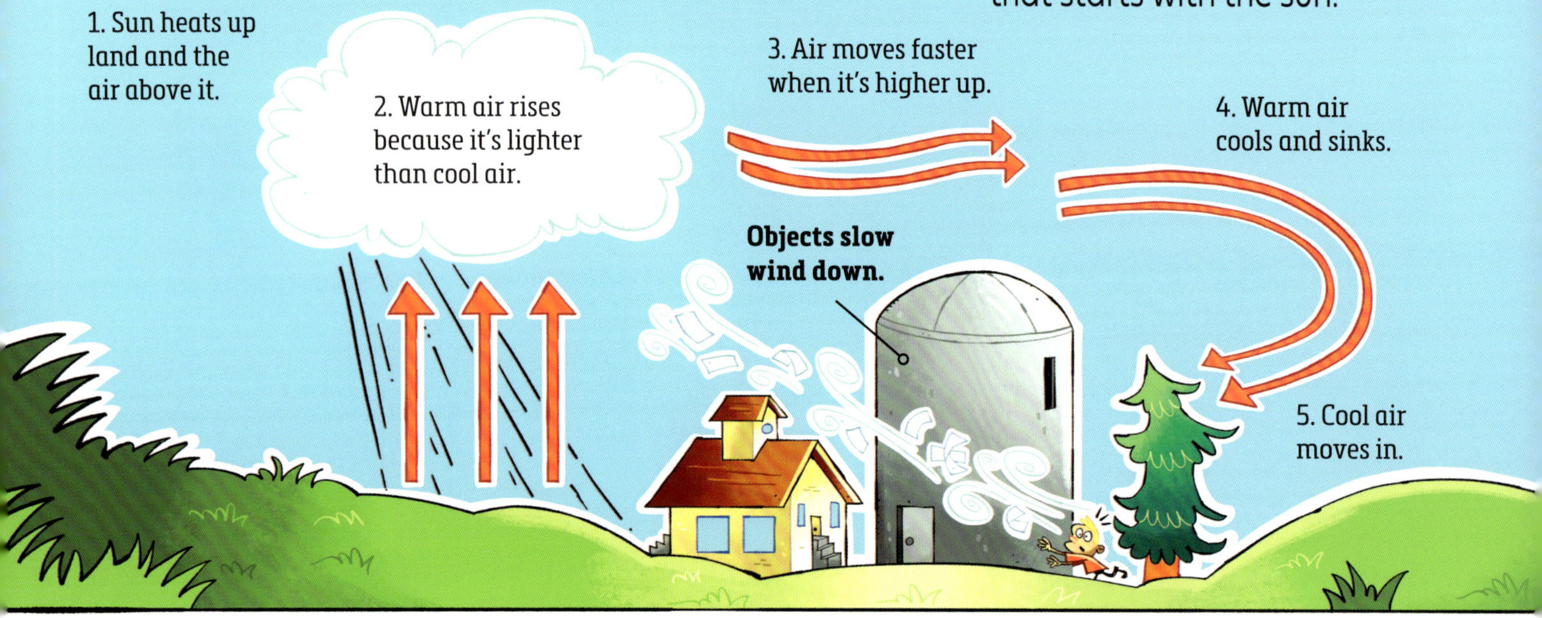

Wind energy is renewable, because winds will always blow. It's clean too, because it doesn't produce CO_2.

Wind energy has been used for centuries:

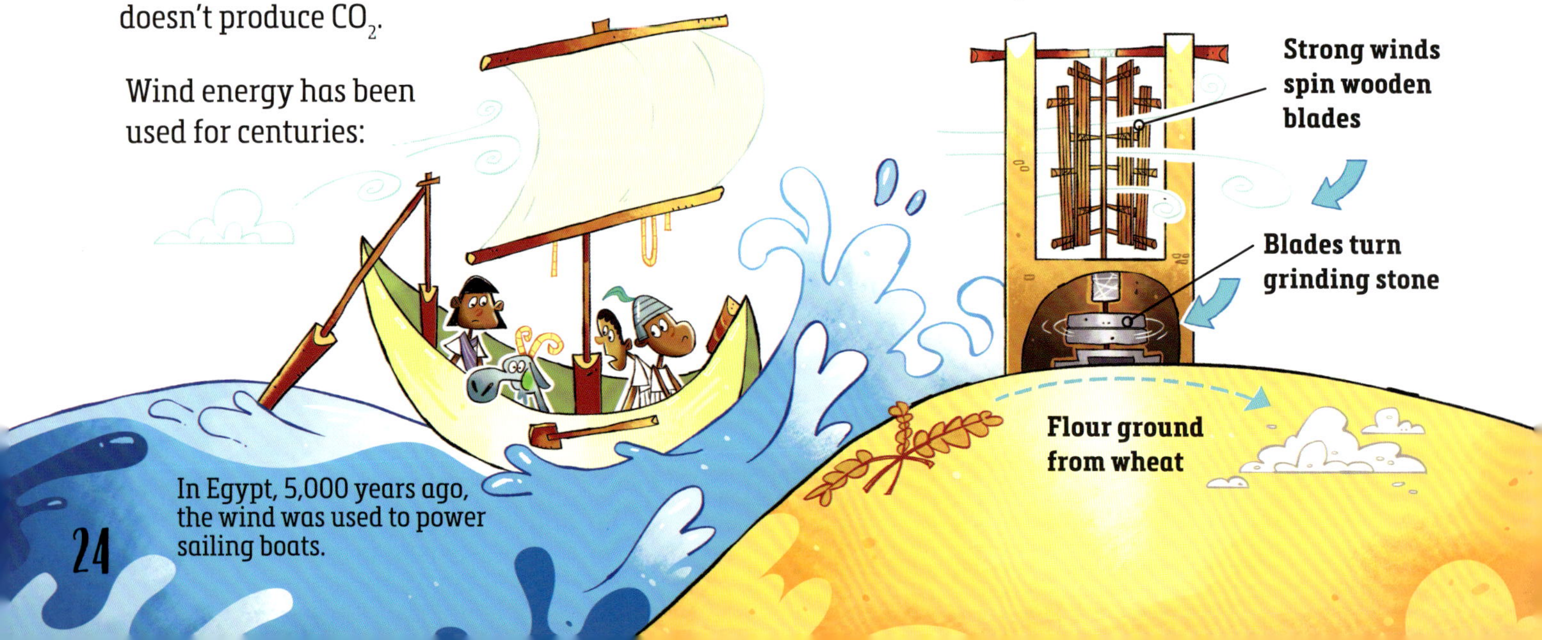

In Iran, Nashtifan windmills have been grinding corn for 1,000 years.

In Egypt, 5,000 years ago, the wind was used to power sailing boats.

The world's first wind machine, called a turbine, was invented in 1887 by Professor James Blyth. It powered his Scottish cottage. When Blyth offered to share his invention with local villagers, they were horrified.

Today's turbines are much bigger and produce lots more energy.

Did you know ...
The tallest turbines are ***918 feet (280 m)*** high and each one can power ***20,000*** homes for a year.

How a wind turbine works:

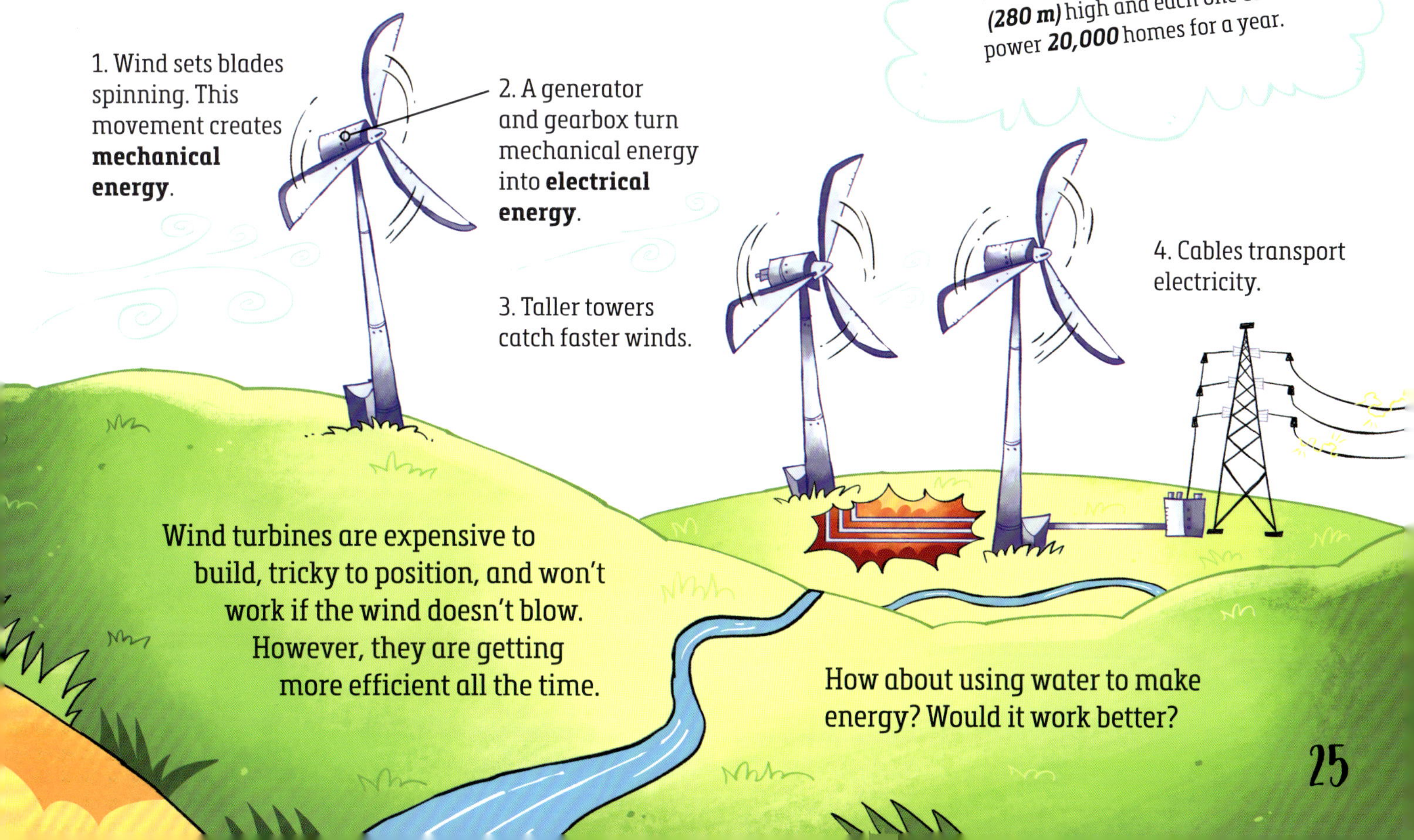

Wind turbines are expensive to build, tricky to position, and won't work if the wind doesn't blow. However, they are getting more efficient all the time.

How about using water to make energy? Would it work better?

WATER WORKS

Water energy, or hydropower, can generate a lot of electricity. Hydroelectric dams are often huge!

Power fact:
Three Gorges Dam in China is ***1.4 miles (2.3 km)*** wide.

How waterpower works:

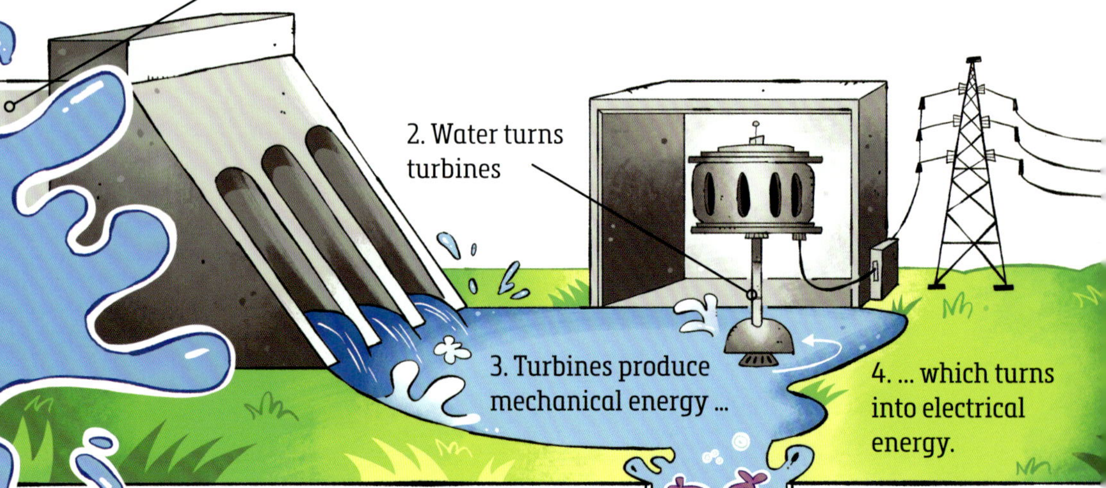

Did you know ...
About ***16 percent*** of the world's electricity comes from hydropower. It's clean, cheap (once it's built) and can work all day.

But some people hate hydro ...

Dams can ruin river systems, destroying plant and animal habitats. Young fish that can't swim upstream are sometimes transported by truck!

Dams produce greenhouse gases from dead plants trapped in dam water.

Is sea power safer?

We can capture mechanical energy from the swell of the sea when tides change. Here's the world's newest, most powerful tidal turbine, the Orbital O2:

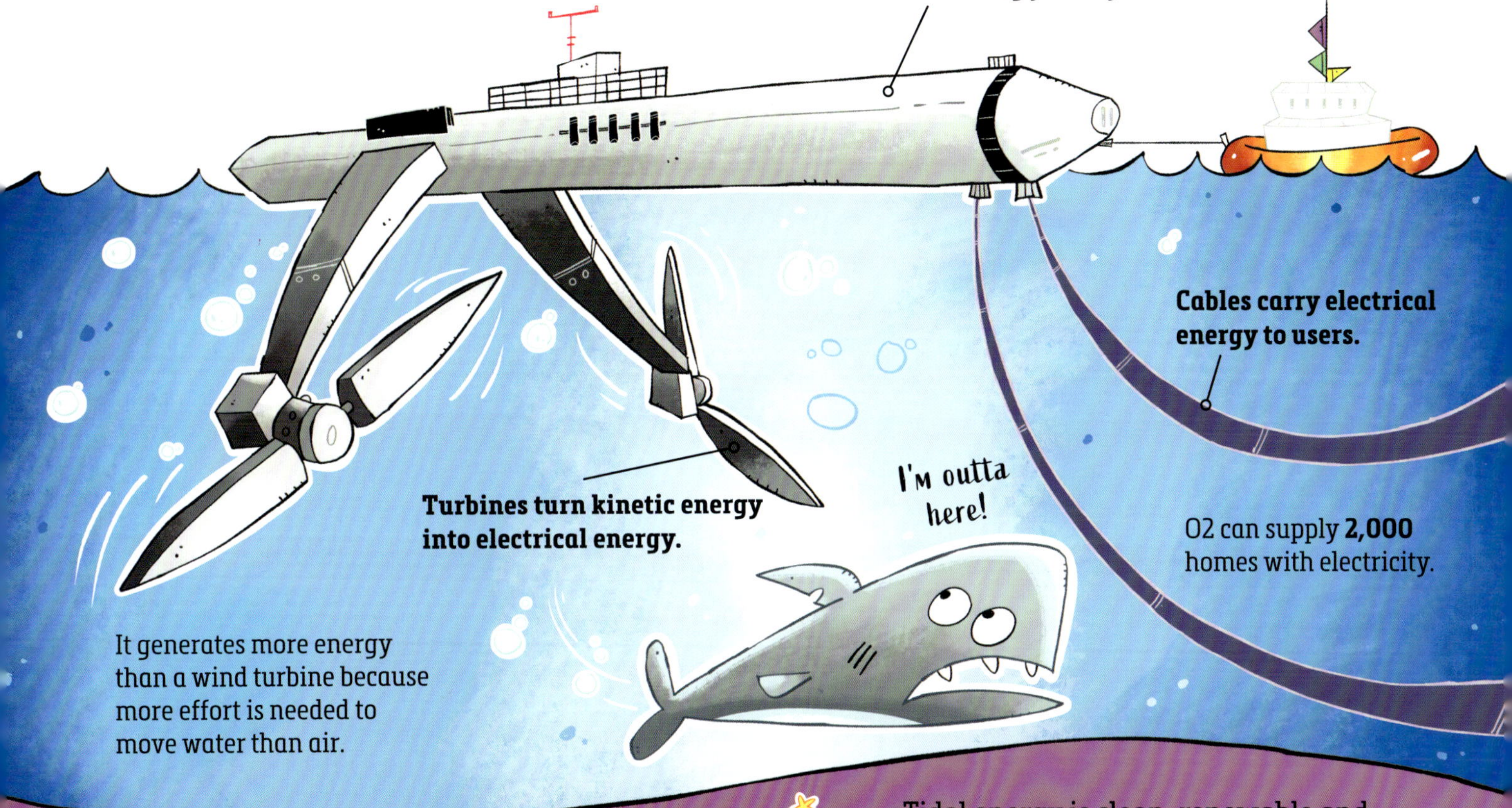

O2 can supply **2,000** homes with electricity.

It generates more energy than a wind turbine because more effort is needed to move water than air.

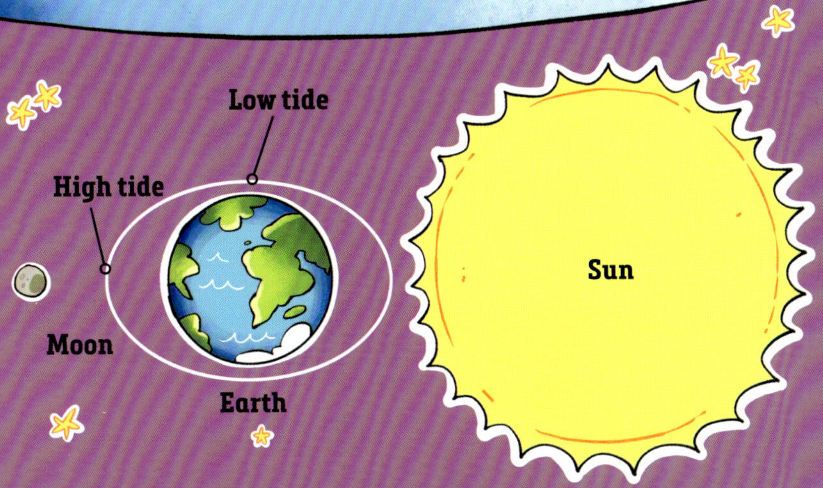

Tidal energy is clean, renewable and doesn't need storage. It's more reliable than wind and solar. Why? Because, unlike sunshine and wind, we know when tides will happen – they follow the daily movement of Earth in relation to the sun and moon.

But there are more forms of renewable energy to explore ...

FAREWELL, FOSSIL FUELS

Iceland uses hydropower with geothermal energy – heat that comes from underground – to produce 100 percent of its electricity!

Natural hot water geysers heat **90 percent** of Iceland's homes.

Iceland can access this underground heat because of its position on Earth.

Two of the twelve tectonic plates that make up Earth's crust meet here. So heat from inside Earth is closer to the surface.

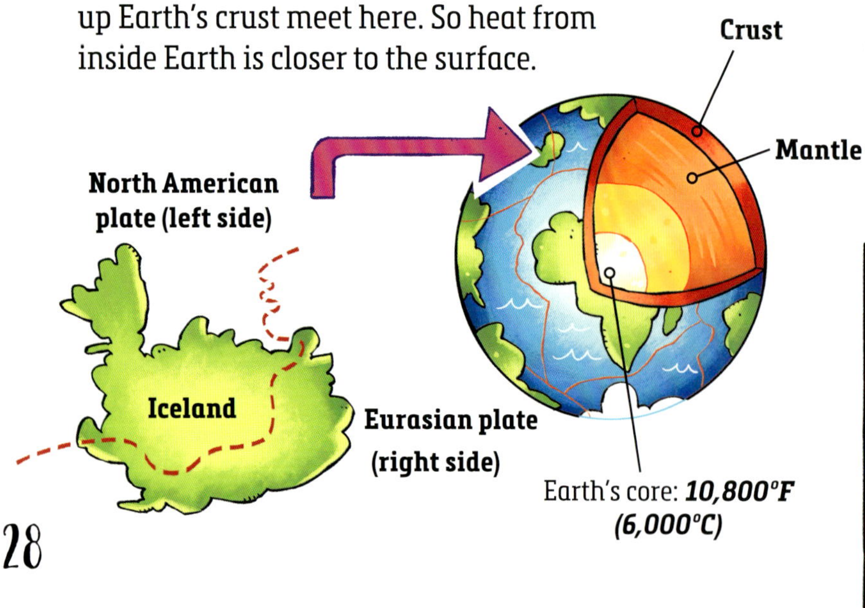

What is geothermal energy?

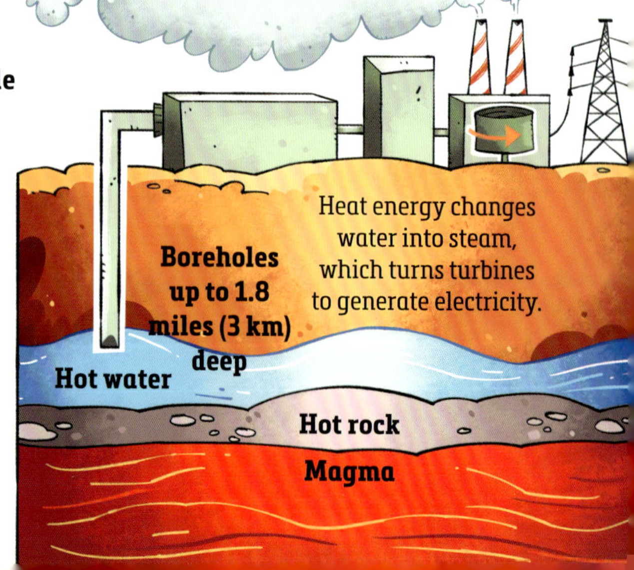

The future of energy

To protect the planet, many countries have set a target year for when they will stop using fossil fuels (see pages 16-17). Iceland's target is 2040. Most other countries are aiming for 2050 or later.

Countries will only reach these targets by switching swiftly to different forms of clean, renewable energy. Progress is already being made:

- China is building a wind farm big enough to power **13 million homes.** It will become the largest wind farm in the world.
- Indonesia is developing geothermal energy, with the help of Icelandic experts.
- Wind and solar provide **10 percent** of the world's electricity, and that figure will keep rising.

The good news is that, even without fossil fuels, there is no shortage of energy on Earth. We can't create more energy, but we won't destroy what we already have. If we can harness it safely, we can use it to provide all the power we need.

GLOSSARY

aerial – a metal rod that receives signals, e.g. to receive a TV channel

architect – someone who designs and plans the building of structures

atmosphere – the gases that surround Earth

atoms – tiny particles that stick together to make everything on Earth

carbon dioxide (CO_2) – one of the greenhouse gases that protect the planet from the sun's heat. Too much carbon dioxide (as well as other gases) in the atmosphere is trapping heat and warming the planet.

chain reaction – a series of events, or reactions, each one triggered by the previous event or reaction

current – air or water moving in a specific direction; a flow of electricity

electron – tiny particles of matter that have a negative charge (see negative charge)

evaporate – when a liquid turns into a gas

force – forces, such as gravity, push or pull an object in a certain direction

fossil fuel – e.g. coal, oil, or gas. Fuels produced from what's left of plants and animals that died millions of years ago.

generate/generator – to produce power/a machine that produces electricity

geyser – a jet of steam that shoots up through a natural hole in Earth's surface

greenhouse gas – CO_2 and other gases that trap the sun's heat to keep Earth warm

habitat – where an animal or plant naturally lives

harness – to control something so that it can be used

hydropower – electricity generated using the power of water

kinetic energy – the energy something has when it is moving

magma – liquid rock inside Earth

molecule – a molecule occurs when two or more atoms join together

negative charge – electrons. When an atom has more electrons than protons (positive charge) it has a negative charge.

particle – a tiny piece of matter

plankton – tiny animal (zooplankton) or plant life (phytoplankton) that are eaten by other sea creatures. Phytoplankton survive through photosynthesis.

positive charge – protons. When an atom has more protons than electrons (negative charge) it has a positive charge.

potential energy – the energy something has because of its position, electric charge, etc, when it is not moving

radiation – objects that give off a lot of radiation are called radioactive. Radioactive objects can hold a lot of energy, and this can be dangerous.

renewable energy – a natural type of energy, such as wind or solar, that does not damage the atmosphere and will never be used up

reservoir – a large lake or tank that stores and supplies water

transform – to change, e.g. from one type of energy to another

transmit – to send, e.g. a TV show

turbine – a machine containing a wheel that produces power through heat energy

upstream – moving against the flow of a river, towards its source

uranium – a type of metal found in rock that can be split apart and used as nuclear fuel

FURTHER INFORMATION

Books

Alternative Energy (series) by Louise Kay Stewart (Wayland, 2023)
Earth's Amazing Cycles: Energy by Jillian Powell (Enslow Publishing, 2026)

Websites

More lightning facts and pictures:
kids.nationalgeographic.com/science/article/lightning-

Lots of information on how the body uses fuel for energy:
www.bbc.co.uk/bitesize/topics/zjr8mp3/articles/ztfcvwx

Take a closer look at geothermal energy in Iceland:
thekidshouldseethis.com/post/geothermal-energy-iceland

INDEX

animals 9, 10, 16, 17, 26
atmosphere 15, 19
atoms 20, 21

batteries 6, 13, 14, 19
brains 8, 9

cables 5, 18, 20, 25, 27
climate change 12, 17
clouds 13

dams 26

Earth 7, 9, 10, 15, 16, 17, 27, 28, 29
earthquakes 21
electrons 5
energy
  chemical 4, 6, 8, 9, 10, 18, 19
  electrical/electricity 5, 6, 9, 11,13, 15, 16, 17, 18–19, 20, 22, 25, 27, 28, 29
  heat 4, 5, 10, 11, 13, 15, 16, 17, 18, 19, 20, 28
  kinetic 5, 6, 7, 9, 18, 27
  light 4, 9, 10, 11, 15, 16, 19
  mechanical 6, 8, 19, 25, 26, 27
  non-renewable (see fossil fuels)
  potential 5, 7, 8, 9, 10, 15, 18
    gravitational potential energy 7
  renewable 21, 27, 29
    geothermal 28, 29
    solar 22–23, 29
    water 25, 26–27, 28
    wind 23, 24–25, 27, 29
  sound 4, 15, 18, 19
  storing 5, 6–7, 19, 23, 27
  wasting (vampire energy) 19

fire 11
food 4, 5, 12, 14, 18, 24
  energy from 8–9, 10
forces 7
fuel 5, 20
  fossil fuels 16–17, 19, 28, 29
    coal 5, 16, 17, 20, 21
    natural gas 16
    oil 16
  uranium 20, 21

gases 10, 18
  carbon dioxide (CO_2) 10, 17, 19, 20, 21, 22, 24
  greenhouse 17
  natural gas (see fuel)
  oxygen 10
generators 5, 25
gravity 6, 7

heat 4, 5
homes 5, 11, 14, 15, 16, 18–19, 22, 23, 25, 27, 28

ice 13

light bulbs 9
lightning 11, 12–13, 14–15

magnets 5
molecules 8, 12
moon 27
nerves 9
neurons 9
nuclear power 20–21
  dangers 21
  accidents 21

particles 5
photosynthesis 10
plankton 10, 23
plants 9, 10, 16, 23, 26
  trees 12
power stations 5, 20–21

radiation 21
rain 23

satellites 19
seas 16, 27
smartphones 18
solar cells 22, 23
solar farms 23
solar panels 22, 23
static electricity 13
steam 5, 20, 28
sun 9, 10–11, 13, 17, 22, 23, 27

tectonic plates 28
tides 27
turbines 5, 20, 25, 26, 28
types of energy (see energy)

water 5, 8, 10, 19, 20, 25, 26, 28
waves 21
wildfires 12
windmills 24
wires 5, 22